fishes for your community tank

by dr. herbert r. axelrod

completely illustrated with color photographs

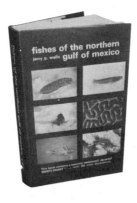

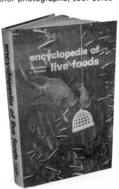

CONTENTS

ISBN 0-87666-072-

Distributed in the U.S.A. by T.F.H. Publications, Inc., 211 West Sylvania Avenue, P.O. Box 27, Neptune City, N.J. 07753; in England by T.F.H. (Gt. Britain) Ltd., 13 Nutley Lane, Reigate, Surrey; in
Canada to the book store and library trade by Clarke, Irwin & Company, Clarwin House, 791 St.
Clair Avenue West, Toronto 10, Ontario; in Canada to the pet trade by Rolf C. Hagen Ltd., 3225 Sar-
telon Street, Montreal 382, Quebec; in Southeast Asia by Y.W. Ong, 9 Lorong 36 Geylang, Singa-
pore 14; in Australia and the south Pacific by Pet Imports Pty. Ltd., P.O. Box 149, Brookvale 2100,
N.S.W., Australia. Published by T.F.H. Publications, Inc. Ltd., The British Crown Colony of Hong
Kong.

The Albino King Cobra Guppies (above) are examples of the modern fancy Guppy. Through the past forty years hundreds of new strains of Guppies have evolved. Dr. Wm. T. Innes photographed the common Guppies below about 1933. These were the fancy Guppies of yesteryear. Dr. Herbert R. Axelrod photographed the King Cobras bred by Mac's Guppy Hatchery.

But not all things have gotten better in the fish world. The famous Innes photo of a pair of Black Sailfin Mollies, taken in 1934, has become tantalizing because huge Sailfin Mollies are almost impossible to obtain. Mollies do not develop sailfins this size in an aquarium. Instead, Black Mollies have been developed in Hong Kong with Lyretails (below), a poor substitute for the magnificence of the "old time Molly." Photo by Dr. Herbert R. Axelrod.

1. A COMMUNITY AQUARIUM?

To the uninitiated, the term **"community"** when applied to a tankful of tropical fishes should mean **a group of fishes that live in peace and harmony together.** To the advanced hobbyist, the term has another meaning. When a group of fishes are kept in the same tank, and this group of fishes complement and supplement each other in terms of eating and swimming habits, and to this group of fishes you add aquarium plants, suitable filtration, heating and aeration, this then is the true meaning of the **"community tank."**

Throughout the aquarium literature you will find several terms which have been invented for the hobby. They don't appear in any dictionary and their meaning has special significance for people keeping fishes.

HOBBYIST—a person who keeps tropical fishes as a hobby.

AQUARIST—another word for a **hobbyist.**

TANK—an aquarium. Plural of tank is **tanks (aquaria).**

AQUARIUMS—this means two or more public buildings in which tanks are maintained. (Chicago and New York have public aquariums.)

AQUARIA—two or more tanks.

FISHES—two or more fish of **different** species or varieties (five Guppies are five **fish**; a guppy and a swordtail are two **fishes.)**

2. WHY A COMMUNITY AQUARIUM?

For the beginning hobbyist who knows very little if anything about fishes, his natural desire is merely an aquarium filled with compatible fishes. He doesn't know which fishes live well together, nor which fishes are to be avoided at all costs. Hopefully his petshop will advise him about which fishes he can add to his present collection; but so many tropical fish outlets now have completely untrained personnel, that this booklet has become a necessity.

Then, too, a community aquarium is more interesting than a tankful of the same species. Not only are the different fishes interesting to watch by themselves as individuals, but their interaction in an integrated community and their different swimming habits, makes them an interesting group.

Many fishes (Swordtails, Mollies, Panchax, Killies, Platies, Guppies and others) swim close to the top. If you closely observe their mouths you will see that they are upturned and open at the top. The Barbs and most Tetras, on the other hand, have mouths that open in the center of their body line, and these fishes can be expected to swim and be active in the middle strata of the water. Then we have the bottom feeders, usually called catfish or scavengers, whose mouths open at the bottom of their bodies, facilitating their poking about on the bottom of the aquarium, digging into the gravel in search of small tidbits of food. Nearly all dangerous fishes are in the group which stay in the middle of the water. The top and bottom feeders are usually peaceful and can be kept with other fishes. (A notable exception are those surface feeders with long, pointed jaws, fishes that look like Pike.)

Every community tank should have a few scavengers. One of the best is the Suckermouth Catfish, **Hypostomus plecostomus**. Photo by Dr. Herbert R. Axelrod.

To help the novice, the following group of fishes is recommended for community groups. The number of fishes recommended is for a ten gallon aquarium which is properly filtered with a suitable undergravel filter. If you use a hipower undergravel filter, add 50% to the number recommended.

3. FISHES FOR THE COMMUNITY TANK.

The following fishes are all peaceful and recommended for the beginner. The points before their name indicates a value in terms of their need for oxygen and space. This number is based upon a **500 base for a ten gallon aquarium.** Thus you can have any number of these fishes providing the total is not more than 500. Should you want only one species, divide the point value into 500 and you can get the amount of fish which can safely be kept in a filtered, aerated ten gallon aquarium. This list is by no means exhaustive and there are hundreds of additional fishes which might be kept in the community tank. See a large book (EXOTIC TROPICAL FISHES by Axelrod and others, about 1000 fishes are discussed and illustrated in color, sells for $20 but is available in every library), for information on other fishes.

A pair of Tuxedo Hifin Swordtails with normal tails. Only the male (upper fish) has the long tail extension. Photo by Dr. Herbert R. Axelrod.

Lyretail Hifin Swordtail. This fish contains two mutant characteristics: the enlarged dorsal fin and the elongated upper and lower rays of the caudal and anal fins. Photo by Glenn Takeshita of Honolulu, Hawaii.

A pair of normal Green Swordtails. This photo was highly retouched and the red stripes on the sides are not as exaggerated in the living fish. Photo by Dr. Wm. T. Innes.

A pair of normal Red Swordtails. The female has the fan-shaped anal fin, while the male's anal is modified into a stick-like gonopodium with which it fertilizes the female. Only the male has the extension on the tail fin. Photo by Dr. Wm. T. Innes.

Points	Name of Fish	Range	Swimming Habits
10	Angelfish, small, 1 ½"	South America	Middle
25	Australian Rainbow, 2"	Australia	Middle
5	Young Betta, 2"		
	(only one male allowed)	Thailand	Top middle
5	Black Tetra, 1"	South America	Middle
10	Bloodfin, 1"	South America	Middle
6	Blue Gourami, 1 ½"	India	Top middle
5	Cardinal Tetra, 1"	Brazil	Middle
10	Cherry Barb, 1"	India	Lower middle
25	Discus	Brazil	Middle
8	Dwarf Gourami, 2"	India	Upper middle
8	Glowlight Tetra, 1"	Brazil	Middle
15	Gold Barb, 1"	Hybrid	Lower middle
5	Hatchetfish, 2"	South America	Top
8	Head and Tail Light		
	Tetra, 1"	South America	Middle
8	Heterorhabdus, 1 ½"	Brazil	Middle
6	Honey Gourami, 1 ½"	India	Upper middle
7	Kissing Gourami, 2"	India	Middle
5	Leopard Danio, 1 ½"	Hybrid	Upper middle
5	Neon Tetra, 1"	Brazil, Colombia	Middle
6	Pearl Gourami, 1 ½"	India	Upper middle
7	Pearl Danio, 1 ½"	India	Upper middle
5	Pencilfish, 1 ½"	Brazil	Middle
15	Ramirezi, 1 ½"	Colombia	Lower middle
6	Rasbora, 1"	Singapore	Middle
7	Rosaceus, 1 ½"	South America	Middle
16	Rosy Barb, 1 ½"	India	Lower middle
10	Scissorstail Rasbora, 2"	Singapore	Middle
10	Serpae Tetra, 1 ½"	South America	Middle
15	Sumatra (Tiger) Barb, 1"	India	Lower middle
8	Tetra von Rio		
	(Flame Tetra), 1"	Argentina	Middle
6	White Cloud Mountain		
	Fish, 1"	China	Middle
6	Zebra Danio, 1"	India	Upper middle

The fishes in this first group are all egglaying fishes. Some, like the Betta, have a bubblenest. Others spray eggs, which may or may not be adhesive, in a random fashion. If they don't eat them, the other fishes will, so don't expect them to have babies in the community tank.

The next group of fishes are the livebearers of which there are hundreds of different color varieties in Swordtails, Platies, Mollies and Guppies.

Livebearers are available in all sizes, from 1" to 5". Don't buy the largest fishes! The reason for this advice is twofold. First, a fish which is over 3" in length is so old that you cannot expect it to live more than one year more. A young fish about an inch will live at least 2 years (barring sickness or accident). The second reason is that the larger the fish the fewer you can keep in one aquarium. And with livebearers, because they are so simple to breed, you'll soon be having your own population explosion if you take the trouble to isolate swollen females in a breeding trap.

The Swordtails, Platies, Mollies and Guppies are all hybrid fishes. None are imported from the wild with the exception of some green Mollies which are caught in Florida. The points are for fishes 1½ inches long. Don't buy larger ones. Grow your own.

Points	Name of Fish	Swimming Habits
8	Swordtails	Top
6	Platies	Top
4	Common Guppies	Top
6	Fancy Guppies	Top
9	Mollies	Top

It is not necessary to have a male for every female. Many successful breeders of livebearers only have 20% of their fishes males; the balance being females. Petshops, however, may charge extra for females since they must buy the fishes in pairs from the farms in Florida where most of the livebearers are bred.

Compare the anal fins of these two fish. Note that in one there is a fan-shaped, normal type of fin while in the other the fin is modified into a fused, large single stick. The male shoots sperm packets at the female with this fin.

A 4 way breeding trap is ideal for isolating Platies or Guppies to save the babies. It is a plastic tank with ventilation and isolates the pregnant female from the rest of the fishes. Photo by Dr. Herbert R. Axelrod.

A trio of Marigold Platies. The female is in the center, with males above and below her. Photo by Dr. Herbert R. Axelrod.

There are many color varieties of Platies. From left to right, top to bottom: Blue Moon, Red Platy, Berlin Crescent, Blue Green Tuxedo, Gold Saddle and Red Tuxedo. Photo by Dr. Wm. T. Innes.

A mutation which first appeared in 1964 was the Red Wagtail Hifin Platy. Compare the size of the top dorsal fin with those above. This fish was developed and photographed by Dr. Joanne Norton.

To sex the livebearers just look at the anal fin. The females have the normal fan-shaped fin you would expect. The male has his anal fin fused into a stick-like intromittent organ with which he fertilizes the female. Care should be taken in mixing Swordtails and their color varieties, with Platies and their color varieties. It has been repeatedly proven that almost any Swordtail will mate with almost any Platy of the opposite sex. The results, while interesting, are not usually attractive. So don't be shocked if your beautiful Blood Red Hifin Lyretail Swordtail has normal Green Swordtail babies!

Not all strains of livebearers breed true. As a matter of fact few of them do, that's why some colors of Swordtails are more expensive than others.

Guppies are probably the most versatile of all fishes when it comes to varieties. Only the male Guppy shows all of the desirable traits of long finnage and beautiful color. While common Guppies may only cost a few pennies each, fancy Guppies may cost 100 times that much.

Each group of livebearers is covered in a separate booklet in the T.F.H. aquarium series. Check these books at your local petshop to get more information on each individual species.

Having covered the middle swimming egglayers and the top swimming livebearers, we have to discuss the bottom swimming scavengers. It is unfortunate that the catfishes are called scavengers because this title somehow insinuates a low quality fish. They are not, and catfishes are amongst the most interesting of all fishes. The **Corydoras** species breed in such an interesting manner that even people who have photographed them cannot decide on exactly what happens.

A group of **Corydoras** will get together and tumble about on the bottom with the female seemingly mouthing the male all over his body. There are usually more than one pair involved in this love play and during the height of the action the female suddenly leaves the group and swims toward the middle of the aquarium where she glues some eggs onto the glass. The eggs have been held between her ventral fins. It is not known where the eggs are fertilized. Did the male fertilize them directly as they were being laid? Or did the female take some sperm in her mouth and fertilize the spot where she pressed the eggs against the glass? No one knows for certain.

The following scavengers are recommended for the home community tank.

Points	Name of Fish	Range
15	Chinese Algae Eater, 2"	Thailand
6	Corydoras species, 1"	South America
6	Farlowella, 4"	South America
12	Japanese Weatherfish, 4"	Japan
5	Kuhli Loach, 2"	Singapore
7	Otocinclus, 3"	South America
10	Plecostomus, 2"	South America
12	Redtailed Black Shark, 3"	Thailand

Two very popular scavengers are the Chinese Algae Eater (above) and the **Corydoras**
(below). **Corydoras** are air-breathing fishes and they swim to the surface every few
minutes for a gulp of air. Photos by Dr. Herbert R. Axelrod.

This page contains photographs of four pairs of Danios. From left to right, top to bottom: Zebra Danios, **Brachydanio rerio**; Spotted Danios, **Brachydanio nigrofasciatus**; Pearl Danios, **Brachydanio albolineatus**; and Leopard Danios, **Brachydanio frankei (?)**. Top photos by Dr. Innes; lower photo by Dr. Herbert R. Axelrod.

Giant Danios, **Danio malabaricus.** Sexing these fish, and all Danios, is simple, since the females become very fat when ripe. Photo by Dr. Wm. T. Innes.

One of the most popular of egglayers is the Tiger Barb (Sumatranus). Photo by Dr. Herbert R. Axelrod.

No fish is safe with any fish more than twice its size. Here we see a female Guppy eating one of her own babies. Normally, Guppies are very peaceful with larger fishes. Photo by Mervin F. Roberts.

It is highly recommended that you include at least 25 points of scavengers in every ten gallon community aquarium. They not only help clean up uneaten food, but they have very interesting and comical habits which add to the entertainment you will find behind the glass walls of your community tank.

WARNING: All fishes will eat fish small enough to be gobbled down whole. Even peaceful Guppies will eat their own babies. So, when gathering your community tank group together, be sure that the largest fish isn't more than twice the size of the smallest fish.

4. MANAGING YOUR COMMUNITY TANK.

There are many booklets written on the subject of **"Beginning the Aquarium"** and **"Tropical Fish as Pets."** Every larger book also has great sections devoted to every topic from water chemistry to the treatment of diseases. If you have a special interest in any of these subjects browse through the books at the library, or buy one at your local petshop. There are almost 200 books on tropical fishes and one or more should answer every question you might have on the subject.

In addition to the books, there are several excellent tropical fish hobbyist magazines. We recommend TROPICAL FISH HOBBYIST for beginners because it is the only magazine with new full color photographs in each issue and has the world's largest circulation . . . and our company, T.F.H., publishes it (T.F.H. stands for "tropical fish hobbyist.") Look through all the magazines at your local petshop and decide for yourself which magazine you like the best; but by all means subscribe to one of them to keep abreast of new fishes and new product development. Enjoy your hobby to the utmost.

There are four basic areas in which the beginner must have some working knowledge: Water (temperature, pH, hardness); Design (plants, cleanliness); Feeding; Aeration. The following sections will deal with each of these categories only with enough information to keep your fishes alive and healthy. If you want more detailed information consult the **Encyclopedia of Tropical Fishes.**

5. WHAT ABOUT WATER?

Water is not the same all over the world. It varies in every locality in pH, hardness and temperature. It also has certain additives such as chlorine and fluorine in certain communities. In order to keep your fishes healthy and happy you must maintain your community aquarium at a pH of 6.6 to 7.6. The pH of the water is the measure of the acidity or alkalinity of the water and a pH of 7.0 is neutral. You can measure the pH of the water with a pH kit. Your petshop has the kits and has the chemicals with which the pH may be adjusted.

Water at a proper temperature and pH is very important. A plastic thermometer inside the tank is a must. A simple pH kit, which is a strip of paper which changes color according to the pH of the water, is so simple a child can work it. Photo by Dr. Herbert R. Axelrod.

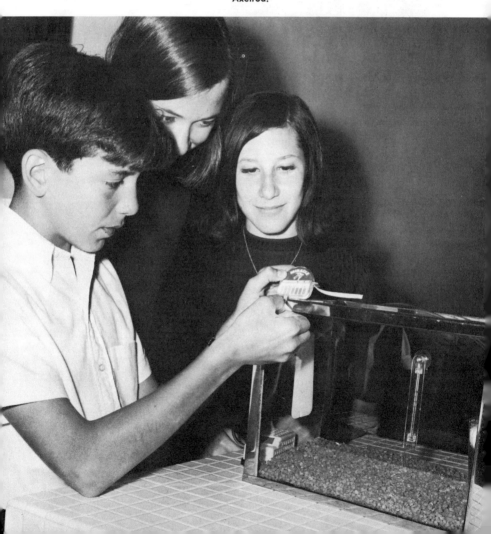

Rosy Barbs, above. Only the male has the intense red coloration on his belly.
Photo by Dr. Wm. T. Innes.

Cherry Barbs are so named because the male turns a deep cherry red when in good condition. Photo by Hansen.

A pair of Common Angelfish with their eggs on a leaf. Angelfishes are available without stripes (Ghost); solid black; half black and with long, flowing fins. Photo by Dr. Wm. T. Innes.

Fishes of the Serpae group comprise many varieties and species. This is a wild pair of Serpae Tetras from Brazil. Photo by Harald Schultz.

If you decide to have a tankful of one species of fish, you are better off to adjust the pH to the requirements of that particular species. Check the pH of the tank from which the fish came in order to decide which is the best pH for the particular species. Livebearers do best at a pH of 7.6 to 8.0. This is especially true of Mollies which develop the shimmies if they are in acid water.

The temperature of the water in the community aquarium should be 75°F. This may be a little warm for the livebearers which would probably do better at 68-72°F., but the tetras like it between 75° and 80°, and they are more sensitive to lower temperatures than the livebearers are to higher temperatures.

The hardness of your water is closely tied in with the pH. Acid water (pH below 7.0) is usually soft and hard water is usually alkaline (ph above 7.0). For this reason it is suggested that you use demineralized water if it is available in very hard water areas. Your local petshop would be having the same water problems that you are having. Check with him and, if necessary, ask him to give you a plastic bag filled with water. Carry the water home in a styrofoam fish box (which the dealer receives from Florida with his consignment of livebearers).

If all of the fishes you buy die within 24 hours, then there is something wrong with the water. Perhaps it is poisoned. There is no disease which kills new fishes in 24 hours. Diseased fishes die a few at a time every day.

You should have thoroughly washed your aquarium in pure tap water without soap or detergent. Your gravel should also have been thoroughly cleaned. If you set up your aquarium and allowed it to stand for a few days before you added your fishes to insure that the chlorine and fluorine left the water and that the water 'aged,' you probably have perfect water.

Step-by-step here's how to set up the tank:

1. Wash the tank with hot water, as hot as possible. Use a paper hand towel to rub all surfaces, especially the inside bottom, to loosen all the fragments of dirt. Pour out the water and rinse the tank as often as possible. If the tank is small enough, do this in your sink. If it is too large, do it outside. You can put the tank on its side and use a garden hose if that is convenient. Even though tanks are cleaned very thoroughly at the factory, they gather dirt during shipment and storage at your dealer.

2. Wash the gravel, pound by pound, either in an open flat pan, or in the tank itself. It is best to wash it in the tank. This insures that both will get a thorough cleaning. After you think the tank and gravel are clean, fill the tank with hot water. When the water cools see if there is any discoloration. If not, then you may proceed.

3. Now all you have is a fish tank and a few inches of clean gravel. Put an undergravel filter in the tank and cover it over with gravel. A hipower undergravel filter is recommended for beginners. This filter is wavy and terraced, sloping from about 2½" in the rear to 1" in the front. By covering the whole thing with 1" of gravel (use

a #3 natural or colored) the tank will have a perfect slope and be as thoroughly filtered and aerated as it is possible to achieve. If you use a regular undergravel filter be sure that the entire bottom is covered. Don't use an undergravel filter which is too small for the tank bottom as the unfiltered area will be the source of contamination.

There are triangular-shaped undergravel filters which are perfect for aquariums in which it is desirable to have the center of the aquarium free and open and which requires a depression in the sand so deep that an undergravel filter is impractical. One interesting design is to put a mirror (seal the back with sealastic cement or an epoxy resin) or piece of shiney stainless steel in the center of the tank with the gravel opened so the steel looks like a miniature pool inside the tank. A small figurine of a man holding a fishing pole as though he were fishing in the mirror pool is quaint.

4. After setting in your undergravel filter you may then put in your plastic plants (live ones are fine, too, but they may be a source of trouble for the beginner . . . add live plants later on). Design the aquarium so the larger, taller plants are in the rear, and the shorter ones are in front. Add the rocks or whatever decorations you may have bought at the petshop.

Undergravel filters are the best filters for most aquaria. The filter goes under the gravel and sucks the dirt into the gravel where it is broken down by bacteria. This is the same principle by which most city water and sewerage are processed. The hipower filter has contours which gives it about 50% more filtration surface, along with an aid to help contour your gravel. There is no undergravel filter which is more effective than this.

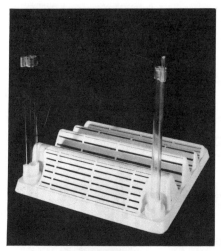

**hi-power
undergravel filter**

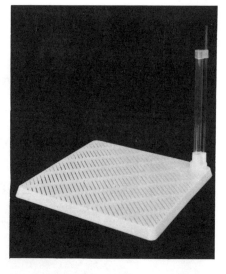

One of the most beautiful of aquarium fishes, the **Rasbora heteromorpha**. Photo by Dr. Wm. T. Innes.

A trio of Dwarf Gouramis. The males are the colorful individuals. Photo by Dr. Wm. T. Innes.

White Clouds are the easiest egglayers for the beginner to breed. Photo by Dr. Herbert R. Axelrod.

One of the most beautiful varieties of Bettas (Siamese Fighting Fish) is the Libby Betta which has fins longer than its body. Photo by Dr. Herbert R. Axelrod.

5. Put your pump into position and hook up your filter, airstone, water wheel or whatever other equipment which requires air.

6. Now be sure that the aquarium is located where you want it to be permanently. Check that the tank is level and that the stand is sturdy.

7. Give the whole tank a final view and then add the water. Don't just pour the water in and uproot all the plants and disturb all of your work. Put a breeding trap or any deep container in the tank and pour the water into that, allowing it to overflow and fill the tank gently.

8. Once the tank is nearly full, give it another inspection. If anything has moved, now is the time to change it. Don't fill the tank more than 75% full at this stage.

9. Turn on the pump and adjust the air valves so all of the outlets are working equally well. Allow the filter and pump to work for a day or so before adding fishes.

10. Hook up your thermostatically controlled heater and place a thermometer in the tank as well. Leave the heater in the water but not plugged into the electrical outlet. After the water in the tank has reached room temperature plug in the heater and adjust the thermostat to the 75°F. setting recommended.

11. Now go out and buy your fishes. Bring them home in a plastic bag and allow the bag to float in the tank until the temperature of the water in the bag is the same as that in the tank. After the temperature has been equalized, open the bag and add a little water from the tank so the pH will be adjusted gradually. If the pH difference between the fishes in the bag and the water in the tank is more than 0.4 you might expect to lose some fishes! Adjust the pH in the tank to that of the fishes.

By floating the fishes in the plastic bag on the top of the tank you raised the water level, thus the reason for not having filled it all the way to the top. After everything is equalized, carefully dump the fishes into the tank, water and all. Then add a little more tap water to bring the water level in the tank to the bottom of the top rail.

12. Be sure that the top of the tank is covered, either with a full hood or a reflector with a tank cover. Leave the light on the tank for the first 24 hours so the fishes can be acclimated and find their own private territory in the tank.

13. **Don't feed the fishes for two days.** When you bought your food you should have gotten some frozen brine shrimp, any kind of dried food, and some Freeze Dried Tubifex. Feed your fishes the freeze dried tubifex worms first. The reason for this is that they like this food best and the food can be measured so the fishes won't be overfed. Then, too, the freeze dried tubifex is the only food for fishes which floats and can easily be removed if it is uneaten. It is also the only food which can be pressed against the glass of the aquarium and stick so you can watch your fishes eat and ascertain that there is no uneaten food left to foul the tank. Feed enough food but don't give your fishes more than they can eat in 15 minutes.

It is possible, after a few days, to begin feeding your fishes from your hand. The freeze dried tubifex worms contains a powerful fish attractant known as "fish nip." This is similar to "cat nip" which is so pleasantly attractive to cats.

6. KEEP YOUR TANK CLEAN.

There are many other types of filters on the market besides the undergravel filters. There are bottom filters, corner filters and outside filters. All are very efficient and bottom and corner filters are recommended over the outside filters because children and cats have been known to knock off an outside filter, thus causing the entire contents of an aquarium to be siphoned onto the floor.

For the larger pieces of accumulated dirt, you should use an aquarium vacuum cleaner which is a plastic tube with a rubber ball. The ball is squeezed sucking the water through the tube and into a cloth sack which filters the dirt from the water and returns the water to the tank.

Siphons are also good and they have the additional value of removing some of the water. It is wise to change about 10% of the water in your aquarium every month. So just siphon 10% of the water off the bottom, dirt and all, and replace it with water directly from the tap. Don't worry about the chlorine or fluorine as 10% won't harm the fishes; but be sure the temperature is almost the same as the water in the tank.

The Redtail Black Shark has a black body and a very red tail. Photo by Dr. Herbert R. Axelrod.

Beautiful Cardinal Tetras, **Chelrodon axelrodi**, attacking a piece of Freeze Dried Tubifex worms which have been pressed against the aquarium glass. Photo by Dr. Herbert R. Axelrod.

The Neon Tetra, **Hyphessobrycon innesi.** Photo by A. van den Nieuwenhuizen.

The Heterorhabdus or Glowline Tetra. Photo by Dr. Wm. T. Innes.

A Three-spot or Blue Gourami. The third spot is the eye. Photo by Dr. Herbert R. Axelrod.

When Siamese Fighting Fishes spawn, the male builds a bubblenest under which he embraces the female. The eggs flow from the female and the male catches them in his mouth. After collecting a mouthful, he transfers them to his nest and cares for them until they are free swimming.
Photo by Zukal.

7. BREEDING YOUR FISHES.

More has been written about the breeding of tropical fishes than on any other aquarium subject. One of the greatest joys of fishkeeping, if not **the greatest**, is breeding different kinds of fishes. The advanced hobbyist competes with his fellow aquarists in trying to be the first to spawn a new import. Many men are world famous for their great finds in the ways fishes breed. The **"Encyclopedia of Tropical Fishes"** emphasizes breeding techniques and divides egglayers into many logical categories.

To get the most of your tropical fish hobby, you should really attempt to breed some fishes, even if you only isolate a swollen female livebearer and wait for her to have babies. Most of them give birth every month, so you won't have long to wait if you get one that looks "ripe enough to burst."

Good luck on your new hobby!

PS-740 MBUNAS (rock-dwelling cichlids of Lake Malawi, Africa), by Dr. P.B.N. Jackson and Tony Ribbinck. Dr. P.B.N. Jackson relates his experiences at Lake Malawi when mbunas were first thoroughly studied. He discusses the habits and habitats of various species in relation to their maintenance in aquaria. One chapter is devoted to an up-to-date list of the mbunas with notes on almost every species. Tony Ribbinck provides an introduction to the behavior of African cichlids followed by separate chapters on the spawning habits of mouthbrooders and substrate spawners. This is an information packed book that treats the most popular group of fishes in the aquarium industry today. 102 color photos, 17 black and white photos, 128 pages.‡ $4.95

PS-718 SHARKS AND LOACHES by Braz Walker is 160 pages of colorful photos and information on almost every shark and loach known to aquarists, including some which just came from China! $6.95.

H-957 NEON GOBIES, by Dr. Patrick L. Colin, is a highly scientific work that has a good deal of interest for marine aquarists as well as ichthyologists and scientific workers in related disciplines, because it is so highly detailed that it provides much information available nowhere else about one of the most popular marine aquarium fishes. . . one of the few that has been spawned in captivity. A truly large (312 pages, 5½ x 8), comprehensively illustrated and painstakingly detailed book of lasting value. Covers all fishes of the subgenus *Elacatinus*. † 250 full color photos and over 100 black and white photos. $20.00

PS-713 FRESHWATER FISHES BOOK 1 by Dr. Axelrod. A true work of art in its highly illustrated colorful majesty, this is the first in a series that will present general information on a family-by-family basis. Almost 650 beautiful color photos, many very large, in this handsomely printed and bound masterpiece. $20.00

S-101 COWRIES by Dr. John Taylor and Jerry Walls. An excellent, comprehensive coverage of the most popular group of seashells, including all phases of their natural history, biology, aquarium care, collecting, and identification. 240 pages of color photographs illustrate all valid cowry species, many of them as living animals. A handy full-color IDENTI-CHART comes with every book. Its low price and extremely colorful format will make it a sure seller. 288 pages with over 400 color photos. $9.95

PS-734 FISH BEHAVIOR: why fishes do what they do. By Dr. Helmut Adler. No other book combines the elements of colorful beauty (more than 100 pages of color photos) with fascinating insight into fishes' behavioral patterns in the same degree as this wonderfully informative and authoritative work. A permanent reference volume of lasting value; big (8½ x 11) in size, big in usefulness, rich in interest and good looks. $17.50

These books available at your local petshop. If ordering direct please add $0.50 ($1.00 outside U.S.) to cover postage and handling.

T.F.H. PUBLICATIONS, INC., BOX 27, NEPTUNE, N.J. 07753

Your name should be on the cover of this magazine

tropical fish hobbyist

If it isn't, mail the coupon

Subscribers receive every issue of TROPICAL FISH HOBBYIST without fail.

Subscribers are kept informed about every important development in the aquarium hobby . . . the new fish, the new people, the new products, the new techniques . . . every month.

They also know that they'll always be up to date with their free supplements to EXOTIC TROPICAL FISHES.

Subscribe NOW to TROPICAL FISH HOBBYIST, the biggest (more pages, more pictures, more information, more readers), most colorful (a minimum of 32 color pages in each issue), most interesting aquarium magazine in the world.